Catlore

CATLORE

Tales from around the World

retold and illustrated by

Marjorie Zaum

Atheneum · New York · 1985

Library of Congress Cataloging in Publication Data

Zaum, Marjorie.
Catlore: tales from around the world.

SUMMARY: A collection of folk tales about cats from
all parts of the world, including "The Magic Ring"
and "Why the Cat Washes His Paws After Eating."
Bibliography
1. Tales. 2. Cats—Folklore. [1. Folklore.
2. Cats—Fiction] I. Title.
PZ8.1.Z29Cat 1985 398.2'45294428 85-7530
ISBN 0-689-31173-7

Published simultaneously in Canada by
Collier Macmillan Canada, Inc.
Text set by Heritage Printers, Inc.,
Charlotte, North Carolina
Printed and bound by Fairfield Graphics,
Fairfield, Pennsylvania
Designed by Mary Ahern
First Edition

To our beloved dog
MAYMAY
"One short sleep past, we wake eternally."

Contents

[vii]

A Note to the Reader

tories about cats have been told for almost four thousand years, for that is how long the cat has been close to man. The tales in this book have been gathered from different countries of the world and are part of folklore tradition. Whenever these stories were told, each storyteller changed his version a little bit to suit his time and place. Usually the beliefs and superstitions of the teller were added to the tale.

Throughout the centuries, cats have been called good, bad, wise, stupid, loyal, treacherous, warm and lovable or cold and independent. In ancient Egypt, cats were revered because they were thought to be sacred to the goddess Isis. Cats were feared and hated in medieval Europe because superstitious people associated them with witchcraft.

In modern times the cat has come into favor again. Mark Twain, the American humorist, and Colette, the French novelist, are among many who wrote about their cats with great affection. There are paintings of cats, books about cats, and cat shows. Many people now view cats with sympathy and admiration.

But all of the different attitudes are only what people have thought about cats, not what cats really are or were. In reality, if a cat is abused, he will become frightened or mean. If he is treated kindly, he will be friendly and trusting.

Time passes, people's beliefs change and folk-lore changes too. A famous scientist has said, "The observer is part of the observation." So it may be that the cat, while being himself, has always been seen in whatever ways suited human purposes. These stories, which come from times long ago and places far away, may tell us something about cats, and something, too, about ourselves.

M. Z.

Catlore

Dividing the Cheese

[A F R I C A]

wo hungry cats stalked out of the jungle. They came to a small village and thought they'd ask for a little food. But the village was empty. Everyone had gone to the festival of the Rain God. As the two cats walked around the deserted village, they saw, in the window of one of the huts, a large round cheese.

"I'm going to take it," said the first cat.

"No, you don't," said the second. "*I'm* taking it."

"Let's not argue," said the first cat. "Let's divide it in half."

"That's good," said the second cat.

"I'll take it," said the first cat, "and *I'll* divide it in half."

"No, you won't," said the second cat. "How

do I know that you'll divide it equally? *I'll* take it and *I'll* divide it in half."

"Let's not argue," said the first cat. "Let's get Tikki the monkey to divide it."

"That's good," said the second cat.

They went to the monkey and asked him to divide the cheese in half for them.

"I'll do that," said the monkey, "but I must have a scale."

They brought him a scale and he cut the cheese. But instead of cutting it in halves, he cut one piece larger than the other. Then he weighed both pieces in the scale. He said, "I didn't divide this too well." He began to eat the heavier piece.

"Oh, what are you doing?" cried the cats.

"I'm eating a little of the heavier piece, to make it even with the light piece," he replied. He ate some of the heavier piece and put what was left of it in the scale.

"Oh dear," said the monkey. "I've eaten a little too much. Now *this* piece weighs less than the other one. He began to nibble on the heavier piece to make it even with the light piece. The cats realized that the monkey intended to eat the whole cheese this way.

"Give us the cheese," demanded the first cat.

"We will divide it ourselves," said the second.

"No," said the monkey. "You might quarrel and then the king of the animals would blame me." He went on nibbling and weighing, first one piece, then the other.

The cats saw there would be nothing left. One said to the other, "It would have been better to have divided the cheese ourselves."

"Go in peace," said the monkey. "And never again let greed destroy your trust in your friends."

The Magic Ring

Li Po, a fisherman, lived with his wife in a tiny cottage by the sea. They had no children, but they did have a cat and a dog whom they loved dearly. Li Po's wife, Mei Hua, took special care of their pets, and the cat and the dog were well-fed and much petted.

When Li Po was young and strong, he caught many fish so there was always plenty of food. But the fisherman grew old, his old bones ached, and he just couldn't work as hard as before. He caught fewer and fewer fish. Soon he and his wife were very poor. Still, they shared what little they had with their pets.

One morning, the old man went out to sea and fished all day without having a single bite. Night was coming and he felt very tired. He decided to head home, even though he hadn't caught anything. Just then, he felt a tug on his line. Quickly he drew it up. There at the end dangled a large carp.

Desperately it pleaded, "Dear fisherman, please let me go back to my home in the sea. There my family waits."

Li Po thought of his own family, waiting for him in a cold cottage with no food. But seeing the sad, round eyes of the carp, he couldn't bring himself to pull it into his boat. So he gently took it off the hook. But before it slipped into the sea, it said, "Fisherman, you shall not go hungry after all. When you pull your boat in, look for a shiny object in the sand. Pick it up, for it is a magic ring, which will bring you everything you want. But you must not show the ring to strangers. Always keep it hidden."

Li Po brought his boat in and looked carefully in the sand. He saw something shining, picked it up, and sure enough, it was a jeweled ring. Another fisherman, sitting nearby, saw him and asked, "What is that, Li Po? What is that you've found in the sand?"

"Just a pretty pebble," answered Li Po, and hid it in his pocket.

As soon as he got home, he whispered to his

wife, "Mei Hua, close all the shutters, then come see what I've found in the sand."

When the room was dark, Li Po showed the magic ring to his wife, his cat and his dog. It glittered in the darkness as though a hundred candles had been lit. He told them how he'd found it and what the carp had said it could do. They marveled at its beauty, but finally the dog said, "Master, we are hungry. See if it will give us food."

Li Po held up the ring and said, "Magic ring of the carp, we are all hungry. May we have food?"

Instantly a table appeared, and on it was a huge bowl of steaming rice, platters of roast meats, delicious green vegetables, sweet honey cakes and tea. Before tasting a morsel, Mei Hua filled the cat's dish and the dog's dish with some of the roast meats. Li Po hid the ring behind a loose brick in the fireplace. Then they all feasted till they fell asleep.

The next day his wife said, "Li Po, why should we continue to live in this tiny old cottage? The sea wind blows through the shutters and through the chinks in the walls. We are always cold. Look at our pets, huddling in the corner, trying to keep warm. Let us ask the magic ring for a better house."

"You are right, Mei Hua," said the fisherman. He took the ring from its hiding place and asked for a larger, warmer house. Instantly a new house appeared, twice as large, made of stone and with a pretty garden.

From that time on, Li Po, his wife, and the dog and cat, had everything they wanted. There was no longer any need for Li Po to fish. He spent his time reading ancient scrolls and painting with ink upon the finest silk.

The villagers gossiped about Li Po's sudden wealth. The fisherman whom he had met on the beach was especially curious. He knew that Li Po was old and couldn't work very hard. He wondered how Li Po had become so rich.

One night the fisherman sneaked up to Li Po's new house and peeked in the window. He saw Li Po's wife, richly dressed and wearing many ornaments. He watched Li Po hold up a jeweled ring and say, "Magic ring of the carp, give me an emerald collar for my cat and a ruby collar for my dog." Two gleaming jeweled collars appeared. Li Po put the emerald collar around the cat's neck and the ruby collar around the dog's neck. Then he carelessly left the ring lying on a little velvet cushion on the table.

The envious fisherman decided to steal the

ring. He waited till everyone had gone to sleep, then quietly crept through the window into Li Po's house. He tiptoed over to the table where the ring, glittering in the moonlight, lay on its velvet cushion. Its radiance illuminated the darkest corners of the room. By its light the fisherman could see bowls and vases of gold and silver, elegant black lacquered furniture, and silk hangings embroidered with dragons and butterflies.

With a trembling hand the fisherman took the ring and hastily wrapped it in a cloth to hide its glowing light. Then he ran home. He told his wife, Shao Ling, what he had seen. The two decided to row their boat to a far-off island. There they would use the ring to gain riches in secret so no one would know. They had no intention of allowing anyone to steal the ring from them.

But they too had a cat, and as they were getting into the boat, she cried, "Please don't leave me! I'll starve to death!"

"Who cares about you?" snapped Shao Ling. "Try swimming across the sea. If you don't drown, I might let you live with us on the island." She and her husband laughed and rowed away.

In the morning Li Po, his wife and dog and cat, woke up and found themselves back in their drafty old cottage. The ring was gone, there was nothing to eat, and they were worse off than be-fore. Li Po had given away his boat when he no longer needed it, so now he couldn't even go out to fish.

"It's my own fault," wept Li Po. "I was warned to keep the ring hidden and I forgot, and now it's been stolen in the night."

"What will become of us?" wailed Mei Hua.

The cat whispered to the dog, "We must think of a way to help them. Rich or poor, they were always kind to us."

"You're right," replied the dog. "We must find the magic ring. But how?" Just then Shao Ling's cat, who had been abandoned, came beg-ging for food. "I see you can't spare a bite to eat," she said. "You are poor again. But Shao Ling and her husband, who have abandoned me, will soon be rich. They've rowed off to a distant island with a magic ring. It will bring them great wealth, they say."

"So they're the thieves," roared the dog, "and they've gone far across the sea. Now we'll never get the ring back!"

"We will get it," said Li Po's cat. "Cats always make plans. Now you, dear dog, will swim across the sea with us on your back, for you are large and strong. When we get to the island, you, dear cat of Shao Ling, will go to their house, for they won't suspect you. But you'll find where the ring is hidden, take it back, and we'll all swim home."

That night when the moon rose, the three friends ran down to the beach. The dog jumped into the water with the two cats on his back. The sea was deep, the current was strong, and there were huge waves. Bitterly cold winds blew, and many times the two cats feared they would fall off the dog's back and drown. But he swam on and on. At last they came to the island where Shao Ling and her husband lived. In the distance they saw a palace ablaze with light.

They lay down on the sandy shore to rest. Shao Ling's cat dipped herself in the water so that it would look as though she had been swimming. Then she ran to the palace. There she found her former master and mistress eating a sumptuous dinner.

"Well, look who's here!" announced Shao Ling to her husband. "But you might as well have drowned, old cat, because I'm not going to feed you!" The cat said nothing but curled up in a corner. As soon as they fell asleep, she got up and began looking for the ring. She searched every room in the palace. She looked under tables, chairs and behind shelves. She opened jars, bottles and boxes. She rummaged in cupboards, in drawers, in closets. The ring could not be found.

Disappointed and tired, she lay down on a pile of silken clothing that Shao Ling had carelessly thrown on the floor. Suddenly she felt a hard object under her paw. It was the ring! But it was tightly sewn into a pocket of Shao Ling's robe.

With her sharp claws and pointed teeth, Shao Ling's cat slowly and carefully broke every thread. Quickly she took the ring and held it in her mouth. Then she leaped out the window and hurried to the beach where the other two were waiting.

"What took you so long?" demanded the dog.

"I . . ." began the cat, but the instant she opened her mouth, the ring fell out, rolled into the sea and was washed away.

"Oh, oh, oh!" they shouted. "Now the ring is gone forever!"

The dog lay down and howled and the two cats cried bitterly.

After a while, Shao Ling's cat said, "We must stop crying and go back. Dawn is coming and if Shao Ling wakes up and finds us here, she'll surely kill us. We must swim home now."

So they trudged back into the icy water. The dog was very tired, and the two cats on his back seemed heavier than before. He felt himself sinking. The waves washed over them all.

Suddenly a large carp thrust its head up out of the water. It was the same carp whose life Li Po had spared. Softly it said, "You have all been loyal and brave. You shall not drown." A small boat appeared and the carp continued, "Get in the boat, it will take you home. When you get to the beach, look carefully in the sand and you'll find the ring again."

The magic boat took them to their own shore. They looked in the sand and saw something shining. It was the ring. This time, Li Po's cat held it in her mouth. The dog was about to ask something, but Shao Ling's cat interrupted, "Don't speak to her!"

They walked home very quietly. Li Po and his wife rushed to the door and greeted them with hugs and kisses. "How empty our house was without our dear ones," they cried.

From then on, they all lived happily together and the magic ring made them rich again. Shao Ling's cat stayed on and became a permanent member of the family. The dog guarded the magic ring in the daytime and at night the two cats guarded it.

Li Po and his wife became very famous all over the land because of their kindness and generosity to all its animals.

Rhymes and Jingles

[ENGLAND]

Great A, little a,
Bouncing B!
The cat's in the cupboard,
And she can't *see*.

K was a kitten,
Who jumped at a cork,
And learned to eat mice
Without plate, knife, or fork.

Come hither, little pussy cat;
If you'll your grammar study
I'll give you silver clogs to wear
Whene'er the gutter's muddy.
No! Whilst I grammar learn, says Puss,
Your house will in a trice
Be overrun from top to bottom

With flocks of rats and mice.
With a tingle, tangle, titmouse!
Robin knows great A
And B, and C, and D, and E,
F,G,H,I,J,K.

Dame Trot and her cat
Led a peaceable life
When they were not troubled
With other folk's strife.
When Dame had her dinner
Near Pussy would wait
And was sure to receive
A nice piece from her plate.

Diddledy, diddledy, dumpty
The cat ran up the plum-tree.
    I'll lay you a crown
    I'll fetch you down;
So diddledy, diddledy, dumpty.

Sing, sing, what shall I sing?
The cat has ate the pudding-string!
Do, do, what shall I do?
The cat has bit it quite in two.

Pussicat, wussicat, with a white foot,
When is your wedding? For I'll come to't.
The beer's to brew, the bread's to bake,
Pussy-cat, pussy-cat, don't be late.

A cat came fiddling out of a barn,
With a pair of bagpipes under her arm:
She could sing nothing but fiddle-cum-fee,
The mouse has married the humble-bee,
Pipe, cat; dance, mouse,
We'll have a wedding at our good house.

Pussy-cat ate the dumplings, the dumplings,
Pussy-cat ate the dumplings.
 Mama stood by,
  And cried, "Oh, fie!
Why did you eat the dumplings?"

Pussy-cat Mole
Jumped over a coal,
And in her best petticoat burnt a great hole.
Poor pussy's weeping,—she'll have no more milk,
Until her best petticoat's mended with silk.

Hie, hie, says Anthony,
Puss in the pantry,
Gnawing, gnawing,
A mutton, mutton bone;
See now she tumbles it,
See now she mumbles it,
See how she tosses
The mutton, mutton bone.

The Fox and the Cat

[R U S S I A]

woodcutter and his wife lived in the forest. They had a cat whom they called Gray Boris. In his youth Gray Boris had been an excellent hunter and chaser of mice. Now he was old and lay by the fireplace all day, trying to keep warm.

One day the woodcutter's wife said, "Peter Ivanovitch, get rid of that cat. He does no work but still eats plenty. We are poor, and I have no more food for him."

But the woodcutter knew that his wife had stored a great deal of food in the shed, which she kept locked. So he said, "Dear Marushka, you know that when Gray Boris was young and strong, he served us well. It is cruel to turn him out now."

"I don't care," answered his wife. "He's only a cat. Get rid of him, or I'll get rid of you."

The woodcutter was afraid of his wife, who was strong and often beat him with a stick. So he gave Gray Boris one last hearty meal, and then he took him deep into the forest. "Good-bye, Gray Boris," he said. "I'm very sorry about this."

"It's not your fault," said Gray Boris with a sigh. "Good-bye."

Gray Boris lay down on the ground and wept. After a while he heard a snuffly sound. He looked up and saw a pair of bright eyes peeking at him from behind a bush.

"Well, come out," said he. "I'm old and weak and can't hurt you."

A young fox came out from behind the bush. "I heard what happened," she said. "It's very sad." Tears ran down her cheeks.

"Now I will die of hunger and cold," moaned the cat.

"No, you won't," said the fox. "Come and live with me in my house. I'll take care of you."

"You are very kind, dear fox," said Gray Boris. They trotted off to the fox's little house.

"If the other animals learn that you're old and weak, they might attack you," warned the fox. "So don't go out!"

"Oh, I won't" said Gray Boris.

One day when the fox was out, a rabbit came

by. He was very curious about whom the fox had taken into her house. He tiptoed into the yard and hid behind a cabbage, waiting to see who would come out. The cat heard him and peeked through the window, but all he could see from that distance was the rabbit's tail. Since he didn't see well anymore, he thought the tail was a mouse. He said, "Hissss! Hissss! Fttt!" The rabbit jumped with fright and ran back to the forest.

In the forest he met the bear, the wolf, and the boar. He told them, "That young fox has taken in a dangerous, ferocious cat! We must all be careful not to offend him!"

"That's ridiculous," growled the bear. "You're a timid fellow anyway. I'm not afraid of a mere cat, and I'll get rid of him."

"But how?" asked the rabbit. "He never comes out. The fox brings him everything he needs. She must be terribly afraid of him."

"Here's what we'll do," said the bear. "We'll have a picnic and invite the fox and the cat. We'll hide in the bushes. When they get here, we'll rush out and beat them up!"

"That's clever," said the wolf. "But where in the world will we get food for a picnic? There's barely enough food in the forest for us!"

"Really?" said the bear." I happen to know

that the woodcutter's fat, greedy wife has stores of food in a locked shed, which she's keeping for herself. We'll steal it, and that will be our picnic. Now, Wolf, you steal the meat and cheese. Boar, you steal the honey, some dishes and spoons, and a tablecloth. And you, Rabbit, go and invite the fox and the cat to the picnic. I'll wait here."

The rabbit went on his errand. As soon as night fell, the wolf and the boar ran off to steal the food.

In the morning the bear spread the tablecloth on the ground and arranged all the food on it. Then they all hid and waited for the fox and the cat to arrive.

Along came the fox and the cat to the picnic. But as soon as the cat saw the tablecloth, he knew it belonged to the woodcutter's wife. When he saw all the meat and pots of honey and even cheese, he was furious. "And she said she had no more food for me! Mroww! Mrroww!"

The bear, who was hiding in the bushes, heard only, "More food for me! More! More!"

"What!" thought the bear. "Here we've gotten together an enormous amount of food, enough for five bears, and that cat wants more! What a monstrous appetite he must have!" He was very frightened and climbed high up in a tree.

Then the cat saw the boar's bristles and the wolf's ears sticking out from behind bushes. Again, because of his poor eyesight, he thought he saw mice. Wishing to impress the fox, he gathered all his remaining strength and jumped as high as he could. He hissed and spit, "Hissss! Hissss! Fttt!"

In a low voice, the boar said, "He shows no fear of us at all."

"Look how high he jumps," whispered the wolf.

"I warned you," moaned the trembling rabbit. "Run! Save yourselves!"

The fox and the cat ate all they possibly could. They took home all the food they couldn't finish. Nobody in the forest ever bothered them, and they lived together for many more years.

So Gray Boris had a happy old age after all.

The Pride of Schildburg

[GERMANY]

he town of Schildburg had no cats, and the Schildburgers refused to believe that cats existed. This was because their town motto was, "If It Isn't in Schildburg, It Isn't." As a result they were lacking in many things, but not mice.

Schildburg was overrun with mice. They ate the grain in the granary, the bread in the bakery, and the pies in the pantries. People from other towns said, "Get a cat!" The proud Schildburgers replied, "If It Isn't in Schildburg, It Isn't."

The mice continued to multiply and grow fat.

One day a traveler carrying a wicker basket appeared at the local inn. "What's in that basket?" asked the curious innkeeper.

"Oh, that's just my cat," replied the traveler.

He lifted a large, green-eyed orange cat out of the basket.

"Cat?" said the innkeeper. "Never heard of it. What does it do?"

"Hmmmmm," said the traveler. "You've never heard of cats? Well, no wonder. They're extremely rare and valuable. This one, for which I paid a fortune, can catch up to a thousand mice a day. Oh, he's a real treasure. I'm never troubled by mice . . . never."

The startled innkeeper removed his apron and rushed to the Town Hall. "Call a Council meeting," he shouted. The Council quickly assembled and the innkeeper told them about the rare, valuable cat that caught up to a thousand mice a day.

"If this is true," said the Mayor, "we'll have to change our town motto to, "If It Is in Schildburg, It Is." And we'll have to persuade this traveler to sell his cat to us."

They hurried back to the inn, saw the cat and begged the traveler to sell it to them.

"No, no!" cried the traveler. "I couldn't sell this cat, this rare, unusual, unique mouse-catcher, I couldn't sell him for all the gold in Spain."

The Schildburgers pleaded and begged for over an hour. Finally the traveler, "out of compassion," he said, consented to part with his cat for five hundred florins. The Chief of Police whispered to the Mayor, "It's a bargain. Grab it before he changes his mind."

The traveler took the five hundred florins and hastily mounted his horse.

"Wait a minute," yelled the Chief of Police, "What does the cat eat?" The traveler, who had quickly galloped some distance away, shouted back, "The cat eats anything you wish." But the Chief of Police thought he said, "The cat eats everything but fish."

"Everything but fish," he told the Schildburgers.

In a short time the mice were being driven out of Schildburg. "What a good cat," people said. "A wonder cat, a marvel. The pride of Schildburg."

When the mice were all gone, the Schildburgers wondered what the cat would eat next. The Chief of Police remembered the traveler's last words as, "Everything but fish."

Another Council meeting was held. The oldest member of the Council said, "Well, if the cat eats everything, first he'll eat all the grain in the granary, then he'll eat the chickens, then the pigs, then the goats, and then—and then—we'll be all that's left. So he'll eat us. That's everything, and that'll be the end of Schildburg."

On hearing this, women fainted, children cried, and strong men grew pale. "Monster!" screamed the Schildburgers. "Horror cat, de-mon!"

The terrified Schildburgers decided to chase the cat out of town before it destroyed them all. Armed with sticks and stones, they pursued him to the river's edge. The frightened cat, who hadn't eaten in three days, jumped in the river, caught a fish and hungrily devoured it.

"We're saved!" howled the Schildburgers. "Schildburg is saved . . . the cat *does* eat fish!"

A Legal Tail

[B U R M A]

In the jungles of Burma lived a strong, handsome and fierce tiger. Wouldn't you think that the other animals would be fearful and terrified of him? But no. Rabbits jeered, deer giggled and monkeys laughed when he passed by.

The tiger was a clumsy oaf who couldn't walk a step without falling over his own feet. Animals who ordinarily would be his prey could easily hear him stomping along, so they had plenty of time to get away. He was reduced to a vegetarian diet, which he hated. But even reaching up for edible leaves, he missed; poking in bushes for berries, he scratched his nose badly; climbing trees for fruit, he fell down. He was getting painfully thin.

Being the laughing stock of the jungle was

very hard to bear, so he took to sulking in his cave. One day his small cousin, the cat, came padding in to visit.

"Hello, Cousin Tiger!" said the cat. Startled, the tiger jumped up, and bumped his head on the low roof of the cave. He had not heard his cousin approaching, so softly did the cat walk.

"Cousin cat," begged the tiger, "please teach me how to walk softly, hunt and catch prey, and in return I'll serve you faithfully for three years."

The cat thought it would be very nice to have a servant for three years, and besides, the behavior of the tiger was embarrassing to the whole cat family. So he agreed.

The very next day the tiger started his lessons. The cat was a good teacher.

"Cousin tiger," he purred, "when one walks, one does not go clump, clump, but places the paw elegantly, delicately . . . so." And he showed him.

"When one hunts," taught the cat, "one crouches down, keeping the profile low in the tall grass . . . so." And he showed him.

The tiger lived up to his part of the bargain. He cleaned the house (the cat was fussy), he cooked the meals (the cat was a finicky eater), he sat with the kittens when the cat went out, and he ran errands.

He was also a very good student. He paid attention, absorbed knowledge, and when there was something he didn't understand, he asked a question. He was learning very well.

"In fact," thought the cat, "he's learning too well. If this keeps up, he'll soon be better than I am. Since he's so much bigger and stronger, I'll be in as much danger from him as the other animals are." He decided for his own safety to leave out one important lesson.

When the three years were up, the tiger humbly asked, "Cousin cat, have I learned everything?"

"Everything," lied the cat. The tiger thanked his small cousin and happily went away.

The tiger now put his lessons to use and began to hunt on his own. But the deer, the wild boar and the bullock all fled before he could pounce. They seemed to know where he was hiding.

"What can I be doing wrong?" muttered the puzzled tiger, as he sat quietly in a bamboo thicket. And then among the cheeps, chirps, croaks and chirrups of the usual jungle noises, he heard a strange whish-whoosh, whish-whoosh, whish-whoosh.

"Now what's that?" wondered the tiger, and he turned and saw his own long, thick tail swishing back and forth, whish-whoosh, whish-whoosh, whish-whoosh. He realized that the animals had been warned of his presence by the sound of his own tail swishing.

"That treacherous, lying cat!" roared the infuriated tiger. "He didn't teach me the most important lesson, namely: How to Swish the Tail Silently!" He jumped up and down in rage but soon realized that nothing would be accomplished by a display of temper. He had to think of a way to punish the cat.

When he felt calmer, he went to the village, and calling out the Headman, demanded to see a lawyer. But the nearest lawyer, the Headman told him, was several miles away in the Golden Valley.

"I'll go there," fumed the tiger, for he now felt very bitter toward the deceitful cat.

Arriving at the house of the lawyer of the Golden Valley, he banged on the door and shouted that he had to see the lawyer immediately. The lawyer, hiding behind the door, sent his servant to say that he wasn't in; for since time began, lawyers have always liked to cause delay. But the enraged tiger charged in anyway, angrily spat out his case, and demanded a lawsuit against the cat.

The lawyer delayed as long as he could, but finally took the case before a judge. The cat was summoned to court and admitted that he had purposely cheated the tiger out of one lesson. He defended himself by arguing that a tiger who knew How to Swish the Tail Silently would be a menace to the whole community.

After careful consideration the judge came to a decision. He said,

"Whereas the cat, deliberately and with malice aforethought, did refrain, refuse, restrict and deny the tiger the benefit of the lesson, namely, How to Swish the Tail Silently, rendering him ineffectual in hunting, and to the contrary notwithstanding the cat having made a bargain, must adhere to it. Because the tiger is unable to revoke his three years service, it is, therefore, the judgement of this court that the cat shall pay the tiger three years' wages. So be it."

The cat paid the tiger but was not obliged to teach the missing lesson, so he never did. While no longer a laughingstock, the tiger has never learned the hidden secret of Silent Swishing and to this day is extremely bitter toward his cousin, the cat.

A Place to Live

[ISRAEL]

he Almighty, blessed be He, gave man dominion over all the animals. But He decided, in His wisdom, that the animals should have a choice in the matter of obtaining their food and a place to live. He called them all before His golden throne and asked, "With whom do you wish to make your home: the farmer, the shopkeeper, or the peddler?" And each animal made his choice. Then the Almighty noticed, waiting apart from all the others, a small, striped cat. In His holy voice, the Almighty called out, "Here, kitty kitty."

Shyly the little cat came forward. Again the Almighty asked, "With whom do you wish to live and receive your sustenance? With the farmer, the shopkeeper, or the peddler?"

"Lord of the Universe," quavered the little cat, "I cannot make up my mind."

"Go then, and try each one," said the Almighty Lord.

The cat went first to the farmer and asked him for food and a place to live. Gruffly the farmer replied, "Give you food and a place to live? Who gives me anything? Earn it, by the sweat of your brow, as I do." And he sent him to the barn to catch mice. When the cat had done all he could he returned to the farmer and said, "I have cleansed your barn."

"Then I don't need you anymore," and the farmer laughed and shut the door in his face. The cold and hungry cat spent the night in the farmer's field.

In the morning he went to a shopkeeper in the town. "O Shopkeeper," begged the cat, "would you have a place for me to sleep, and a way for me to earn my daily bread?"

"Certainly," responded the shopkeeper, who happened to be a fishmonger, "but you must live in the shop and keep it free of mice." The cat agreed. That night the shopkeeper went home to sleep, but the cat stayed up all night in the shop. He frightened the mice away, he fought off a large rat, he pounced on insects, and did everything he could to protect the fish.

In the morning, hoping for a bit of breakfast,

he approached the counter where the fishmonger worked. But the fishmonger shouted, "Get away! Can't you see I have customers? Don't bother me —get in the back room!"

The cat went to the back of the shop to wait for his breakfast. He was so hungry that he began to nibble on a tiny morsel of fish that he found on a shelf. "Hey there!" yelled the fishmonger coming into the back room. "Don't you eat that fresh fish! You eat only stale, rotten fish that I can't sell!" And he gave the cat such a hard kick that the animal went flying out the door.

Hungry and tired, the cat approached the peddler's wagon.

"O Peddler," he cried. "Have you a bit of food for me? And if I keep the mice away, may I have a place to sleep in your wagon?"

Haughtily the peddler answered, "I travel round the countryside selling fine cloth to wealthy people. There are no mice in my wagon, and besides, you might even get cat hairs on my fine silks and satins. I have no use for you. Get away!"

The heartbroken cat appeared once more before his Creator.

"O Lord of the Universe," he said weeping. "There is no place on Earth for me."

The Lord of the Universe replied, "I have

created the Earth to sustain and nourish all My children. Therefore, there must be a place on Earth where My cat may eat and sleep. Try again."

Obediently, the cat returned to Earth. He would try another farmer, another shopkeeper, another peddler. As he trudged wearily through an open field, he became aware of the most wonderful aromas wafting from the window of a small cottage. He smelled baked meats, pies, and fresh cream. Timidly, he approached the house and stood under the window, his nose twitching and his mouth watering.

A woman came to the window, leaned out and called, "Here, kitty kitty." She took him into her kitchen and fed him. After he had eaten, she held him in her lap and said, "Now I will not be lonely anymore. I have a cat."

The cat rejoiced in his heart and soon heard the Lord's voice saying, "Well, My cat, have you found a place on Earth with the peddler, the farmer, or the shopkeeper?"

"O Lord of the Universe," cried the warm, well-fed cat, "there is no place on Earth like the kitchen of a kind-hearted woman. Here I will stay."

To express His pleasure, the Almighty sent

rays of His golden sunshine through the kitchen window.

And so to this day, you can usually find one of His cats eating and sleeping in the sunny kitchen of a kind-hearted woman.

Why the Cat Washes His Paws After Eating

[G R E E C E-*after an Aesop fable*]

t happened that Cat had caught Bird and was preparing to eat him for dinner. Holding Bird down with one paw, Cat leaned over, intending to take his first bite. Bird, who was very clever, said, "Cat, what crude manners you have. How uncouth you are!"

Cat, who prided himself on his elegant taste and impeccable manners, was very offended.

"What do you mean?" he demanded.

"Why," said clever Bird, "everyone knows that animals with clean habits and graceful manners wash their paws before dinner!"

Cat, who considered himself the cleanest, most graceful of creatures, immediately lifted the

paw that was holding Bird, and began to wash.
Bird flew away, chirping and laughing.

Cat lost his meal but he learned his lesson,
and to this day washes his paws after dinner, lest
the dinner fly away.

The Princess of Cattenborg

 poor widow lived at the edge of a large and gloomy forest. All she had in the world was a son, a daughter, a cow and a cat. The mother and daughter worked hard, but the son was selfish and lazy. He loafed around the house, eating all the food, teasing his younger sister and pulling her long blonde hair. But the girl helped her mother all she could, milked the cow and fed the cat.

One bitterly cold winter day the mother grew sick. She called both children to her and said, "Children, I am dying. Long ago, when I was young, we were not so poor. But now I can leave you nothing but this old cottage, the cow and the cat. Be good, and remember me." Then she died.

The two children buried their mother in the forest and returned to the cottage. In a mean voice, the boy said, "This old cottage is falling down, and I'm cold and hungry. So I'm going to take the cow, which is valuable, and sell her. Then I'll have money to set myself up in town."

"But what will become of me?" cried his sister.

"You, dear sister," said her brother with a sneer, "can have the worthless cat, since you always fed him, and were so fond of him." He took the cow and went away.

The girl put her arms around the cat and wept with fear and loneliness. "Dear mistress," said the cat, "you've always been kind to me. Now I will help you. I know how you can find great happiness but you must leave here, follow me, and do exactly as I say."

The girl agreed, thinking that she had no other choice. So she dried her tears, picked up her bundle and followed the cat into the dark forest. The wind moaned, the trees shook and the girl imagined she saw strange, frightful shapes everywhere. But the cat seemed to know where he was going, so she took courage and followed him.

Eventually he led her to a place where there were huge old oak trees with great spreading branches. "I said that you would find happiness if you obeyed me," the cat reminded her. "So do as I tell you, no matter how odd it seems. Take off all your clothes, which are old rags anyway, tear them up and bury them. Then climb high up in the branches of this tree and hide yourself." The girl was surprised but she did as she was told.

The cat then ran to a royal castle he knew was nearby. There he asked for the king, who was so amazed at seeing a talking cat, that he granted him an immediate audience.

"Your Majesty!" cried the cat, "There's been a terrible crime! While my lady, the Princess of Cattenborg, was riding through the forest, she was robbed by a gang of vicious bandits. They stole her jewels, the ruby-embroidered satin gown she was wearing, and a trunkful of other clothes. Now my lady is hiding in a tree and can't come down because she has nothing to wear."

The king was shocked and angry that such a thing could happen in his kingdom. He sent his son to the forest with servants carrying fine clothes for the princess to wear. When the prince arrived, he glimpsed the girl high up in the branches of a great old oak tree. She had wrapped herself in her long blonde hair and he thought her as beautiful as a dream.

The prince sent ladies-in-waiting to dress the unknown princess in a gown of silk. When she was properly dressed the girl came forward and the prince was even more delighted by her beauty. He helped her into the coach, which had been sent to bring her to the castle.

During the ride the cat sat on the girl's shoulder and whispered in her ear: "You must pretend to be a royal princess. When you meet the king and queen, you must curtsey. If the queen asks you anything you can't answer, say only, 'Oh, it certainly was different at home in my beautiful castle Cattenborg.' Say nothing else."

When they arrived at the castle the king and queen greeted her kindly. She curtseyed to them and spoke very properly. The prince told his mother that he wanted to marry the beautiful princess.

But the queen objected. She said to the king, "Sire, how can we allow our son to marry this stranger? We don't know anything about her and I doubt if she's good enough for *our* son! We don't even have proof that she really is a royal princess."

The king replied, "My Lady Queen, you must admit the girl is lovely and charming and has good manners. I can't understand why you're so suspicious."

But the queen decided to put the princess, or whoever she was, to a test. Before her guest dressed for dinner, she sent her lady-in-waiting to the girl with another beautiful gown. But this one had a long train made of satin and lace.

"If she really is a princess," said the queen to her maid, "then she'll be accustomed to fine clothes and will know how to walk in a dress with a train. Otherwise, she'll trip and fall over it. And then we'll know the truth."

The cat, who had been hiding under a chair, heard this and ran to warn his mistress. "Hold the train over your right arm," he instructed her, "and walk tall and gracefully." He rushed back to the queen's rooms and concealed himself again. He heard the queen tell the Master of Ceremonies, "A royal princess would know that at dinner, we use silver cups with the first course and golden cups with the second course."

It was too late for the cat to warn his mistress. The other guests were already seated at the long dining table in the great hall. But when the girl came down the stairs, walking tall and holding the satin and lace train gracefully over her right arm, no one doubted that she was a royal princess.

As soon as she was seated the queen suggested that she taste the wine. Thinking the golden cup more elegant she began to reach for it when she felt a sharp scratch on her ankle. "Oh!" she cried.

"What is it?" asked the Prince.

"Oh, it certainly was different at home in my beautiful castle Cattenborg," answered the girl, but she knew that her cat had warned her not to take the golden cup. So she lifted the silver one. The prince glanced at his mother as if to say, "I knew she was a princess all along."

The queen was not convinced. She whispered to her lady-in-waiting, "Well, she does seem to have royal manners, but I'm just not satisfied. I must have more proof, since my son wants to marry this girl."

Later that night, the queen stealthily crept into the bedroom she had given the girl. But the cat was crouched behind the long velvet drapes and saw the queen place a straw beneath the mattress.

"A princess is extremely sensitive, so if she really is one, she'll be very uncomfortable tonight," the queen laughed. "We'll soon know."

The next morning the queen asked the girl if she had slept well.

"As well as I could," replied the girl, "but I'm black and blue all over. I felt as though there were a tree under the mattress. It certainly was different at home in my beautiful castle Cattenborg!"

Now the queen had no more objections to the marriage. She made preparations for the journey to the castle Cattenborg, since a royal princess should always be married from her own home.

"When shall we leave, my dear, and how far is it to your castle Cattenborg?" asked the queen. The girl couldn't answer anything at all, but the cat quickly replied, "We can start tomorrow morning."

In the morning everyone assembled in the courtyard. There were coaches, horses, knights, noble ladies, servants and wagons loaded with provisions for the trip. The king's banners, purple with silver fringe, flew in the cold wind. Trumpets blared, and the procession began.

They traveled far into the dense forest. At twilight they came to a part of the countryside that was feared by all. Many years before, a horrible troll had murdered a noble family living in a nearby castle, and there, in stolen splendor, he still lived. Every night he roamed this part of the countryside, killing, stealing, and destroying. He was hated and feared, but no one could harm him. However, he could not travel far from the castle for the sun was his enemy. If he looked straight into the sun, he would burst, so he always returned to his castle before sunrise.

Since it would soon be night the royal party decided that it was safer to camp than to travel on in the dark. Tents were set up and sentries were posted. As night fell, the sentries shivered and drew closer together.

Alone in her tent with her cat, the girl was nervous, but not only because of the troll. "What shall we do?" she cried, "There is no castle Cattenborg! Where are you leading us?"

The cat replied only, "Trust me." He knew that the troll's castle was nearby.

So when everyone was asleep, the cat stole into one of the tents and took several candles and some matches. Then he ran as fast as he could through the forest, intending to reach the troll's castle before sunrise.

When at last he arrived at the castle, the night was still dark—but there was a faint glow in the eastern sky. The cat lit a match and melted the wax from the candles into a soft ball, which he stuffed into the keyhole of the castle door. Then he climbed up an old oak tree and hid in its leafy branches.

In another moment the troll came pounding through the forest. He was late this morning. He had spent most of the night sitting on a low hill, observing the royal wedding party camped at the edge of his domain. Because of his curiosity he had forgotten the time, and now it was too late to kill anyone or destroy anything. The sun was coming up and he had to get inside the castle quickly. Angrily he pushed his key into the keyhole. But something stopped it. The wax had hardened and the key could not go in. The troll flew into a rage and began to scream.

As the sun rose, the cat, from his perch high in the tree, called out, "Oh, troll!"

The troll turned toward the cat, faced directly into the sun and burst. Little pieces of troll sizzled and burned up into ashes, which the wind blew away. The castle was free.

Late the next day, the royal procession arrived at the castle. The cat told them, "This is the castle Cattenborg. Many years ago a horrible troll killed the noble family who lived here, and took possession of their castle. But the noble lady disguised herself as a nursemaid and escaped with her little boy and her newborn baby girl, hidden in a cat's basket. My mistress was that baby girl and she is descended from the noble Cattenborg family. She is truly the Princess Cattenborg."

Everyone was overjoyed. There was a grand

wedding with great feasting, music and dancing. The prince, the princess and their loyal cat lived many happy years in the beautiful castle Cattenborg.

Folk Sayings

If a cat sneezes, you may expect rain.

Rub a cat's paws with butter and it will never leave home.

To keep a stray cat, let it see itself in a mirror.

It is good luck to dream of cats.

If a cat jumps on you in your dream, you'll receive money from a relative.

A cat washing his face in front of a door is a sign
of company.

Make a wish when looking at the paws of a gray
cat, and the wish will come true.

It is very lucky to have a gray cat pass in front of
you.

A cat following you home indicates good luck.

You will always be lucky if you know how to make friends with strange cats.

The girl who is anxious to be married should feed a cat from her old shoes.

The first person a cat looks at after washing its face will be the first one to marry.

The girl who finds a strange cat in her bedroom at night will be lucky in love.

Count Gatto

[I T A L Y]

rich and important cat lived in a small Italian village. He was a counselor to the king and had been given the title of Count Gatto.

He and his wife lived in a white stone house. Its windows were made of colored glass. Count Gatto's wife scrubbed the white stones till they gleamed, and polished the colored glass windows till they sparkled. They had a flower-filled garden, which they tended very carefully. They were proud of their home, and as cats do, kept everything very clean.

The two cats lived happily together and one day the wife gave birth to five beautiful kittens. Each one had long silver fur and glowing emerald eyes. Unfortunately, the little mother became sick and died. Count Gatto was left alone with five tiny silver kittens. He couldn't care for them by himself, so he posted an advertisement on the wall of the Town Hall. It read:

W A N T E D
A Young Girl With
A Kind Heart
To Care For
Poor Motherless Kittens
Must be Neat & Clean.
Large Reward for Good Service.
Apply to Count Gatto.

In the same village there lived a widow with two daughters. Elena, the elder, was very pretty, with long golden hair, pink cheeks, and large blue-gray eyes. She was very conceited, however, and would do nothing all day but sit and admire herself in a mirror. The younger daughter, Maria, was not thought to be pretty but she had a cheerful smile and sparkling eyes. Because her older sister thought herself too grand to do housework, Maria had to do twice as much. But she did it without complaining.

One morning the widow passed the Town Hall and saw Count Gatto's advertisement. "Ah! Reward!" she thought. "Reward! My Elena could dazzle that rich cat with her beauty and bring home a large reward! As for the kittens, pooh! Anyone can take care of kittens." She rushed home to tell her daughter.

The next day Elena and her mother hurried to see Count Gatto. When they arrived, he told them that soon he would have to travel to a far country on the king's business and needed a reliable girl to care for the kittens in his absence. Elena agreed to stay and do all that was necessary. Count Gatto packed his suitcase and left.

Elena lived in Count Gatto's house for a month. In all that time she paid no attention to the kittens. When they came to her for petting she kicked them away. Once a day she threw them some stale scraps of food. Their long silver fur grew dirty and matted, but Elena never combed them. She was too busy combing her own long golden hair and looking at her reflection in the colored glass windows.

The white stone house turned gray, but Elena never scrubbed the stones. The colored glass windows were covered with grime, but Elena never washed them. She had found a large mirror and could see herself better in it than in the windows. The kittens sickened and became so weak they could barely crawl. They lay in a cold corner and coughed, mewed and cried all day. Elena ignored them. She spent her time thinking about the large reward.

One stormy night Count Gatto unexpectedly came home. His house was dirty, the windows grimy and the garden unkempt. He threw open the door and saw his dying kittens lying on a filthy mat in a drafty corner. He turned to Elena in a rage.

"Get out!" he shouted. "Leave my house and never come back!"

"What!" exclaimed Elena. "I've been here a month, as we agreed. Give me my large reward!"

"Here is your reward," said Count Gatto, and he put out his long sharp claws and scratched her arm. Then he threw her out into the storm. Elena ran home crying.

Count Gatto gave his kittens food and medicine. The kittens regained their health, though they were still very thin. He cleaned his house inside and out. But the Count was worried, for he knew that he would have to make another trip soon and the kittens were still a bit weak.

He put up another advertisement. This time it read:

W A N T E D
A Young Girl With
A VERY KIND HEART
To Care For
Poor Motherless Kittens
Must Be Plain-Looking,
Very Neat & Clean.
Reward for Good Service.
Apply to Count Gatto.

The next day the widow and her daughter Elena passed the Town Hall and saw the new advertisement.

"Well!" said Elena. "Plain-looking! That certainly fits Maria. And I think she should go to the Count's house and claim the large reward *I* worked so hard for!"

That afternoon the plain-looking Maria went to Count Gatto's house and applied for the job. She didn't tell him that she was Elena's sister. She thought he wouldn't hire her if he knew and then her mother and sister would be angry with her.

Count Gatto showed the kittens to Maria. She was filled with pity when she saw how thin and weak they were, and she kneeled down on the rug where they lay and kissed them. Count Gatto then asked her to stay for a month. Feeling better, he packed his suitcase and left.

The first thing Maria did was cook a meal of foods especially good for kittens. Then she combed each kitten's long silver fur. She washed the rug they had been lying on and dried it in the sun, so that it would be clean and fluffy. While the kittens were napping, she cleaned the house. In the evening she cooked another wholesome meal for them. Then she played games with the kittens till bedtime.

In the morning she took them out to the garden for sunshine and fresh air. As time passed the kittens slowly became fatter and healthier.

Soon the month was up. Count Gatto came home. Five lively kittens, purring loudly, bounded to the door to greet him. His house was bright, clean and orderly and Maria had prepared a nice supper of foods especially good for older cats. Count Gatto was delighted. He praised Maria and handed her a large silver chest.

In the chest was a gown of emerald green velvet, the same color as the kitten's eyes, embroidered all over with silver flowers and leaves. Count Gatto told Maria that it had once belonged to a great queen. Maria was so overwhelmed she couldn't even try it on.

"I'll give it to Elena," she thought. "She is so beautiful, it will suit her." But she thanked Count Gatto, kissed the kittens goodbye, promised to visit, and went home.

Elena took the gown and put it on. "After all, it's mine, I earned it," she said, and didn't even thank Maria.

Some weeks later a festival was to be held in the village. The young prince had promised to attend and the village girls hoped that he would choose a bride from among them. The girls and their mothers had been sewing, primping and fussing for a month in advance. Every girl hoped to look her best on the festival day.

When the prince arrived he immediately went to see his old friend Count Gatto. He praised the count's happy, healthy kittens and admired the beautiful house. The count was pleased and told the prince the story of Elena and Maria, for now he knew that they were sisters.

"And so," he concluded, "I gave Maria the emerald velvet gown. She'll surely wear it to the festival, so you will know who she is."

"She's a kind, sympathetic girl," said the prince. "How different from the ladies of the court, who don't care about anything but themselves. Maria is the girl I'll ask to be my wife. I'll

[66]

look for the girl in the emerald velvet gown." He stepped into his golden coach and ordered the driver to take him to the festival.

But the Prince's servants, who had run on ahead, whispered and gossiped to all the people they met. "Count Gatto has told the prince about the good Maria, daughter of the widow. The prince will ask Maria to marry him," they said.

"Ah!" said the ladies of the village, "we must tell the widow of this." They all ran to the widow's house, stumbling over each other to see who would get there first with the news.

When the widow saw the prince's coach approaching, she said to Elena, "Go, put on the gown of emerald velvet and hurry to the festival. He will think you are Maria and you will marry the prince."

Elena dressed in the gown and fluffed out her long golden hair. She was so pleased with her image she could hardly drag herself away from the mirror. Her mother had to push her out the door and rush her to the festival.

The prince, looking out over the crowd, saw the golden-haired Elena in the emerald velvet gown. "Dear Lady," he said, "how beautifully your golden hair shines in the sun! But your character shines even more brightly. Count Gatto has told me how kind you were to his poor, motherless kittens." Then he asked Elena to marry him and she consented. Maria stood in the shadows and said nothing.

The wedding party set out in the golden coach. Maria and her mother, who were to be guests at the wedding, sat opposite the prince and Elena. When they came to Count Gatto's house, five silver kittens rushed out to greet them. Elena quickly threw a veil over her face and held out her arms to them. But the kittens hissed at her and scratched her and cried out at her touch. They all scampered into Maria's lap.

"I see," said the prince, "that a pretty gown hides a cruel heart. But the kittens aren't fooled by fine clothes. They fear the girl with the golden hair. The plain girl with the cheerful smile and sparkling eyes is the one the kittens love. She is the girl I'll marry."

After ordering Elena and her mother out of the coach, he rode off alone with Maria. After their marriage, Maria and the prince made many visits to the house of Count Gatto, while the kittens continued to grow up and even had kittens of their own.

The Faithful Cat

ong ago, in the city of Osaka, there lived a wealthy man with a beautiful fifteen-year-old daughter. O-Toyo's lovely face and gentle manner made many young men wish to marry her, but she was not interested in any of them. She spent her time reading, embroidering, or sitting by the river, always accompanied by her pet white cat, Snowflake.

O-Toyo fed the cat choice morsels of food from her own plate. Often she held him in her lap, combing his soft white fur with a silver comb. Snowflake followed O-Toyo, purring and rubbing his head against her. They were always together.

O-Toyo's mother had died some years before. Her father then brought his sister to live in the house and take care of his little girl. But as

O-Toyo grew up, her aunt became more and more jealous of the girl's beauty. She herself was very beautiful, and not old, but compared with O-Toyo, she looked dull and haggard. She was anxious to get rid of her niece.

So she went to her brother and said, "Now see here, Honorable Brother! It's high time O-Toyo was married. Do you not want grandchildren? Why is a girl of O-Toyo's age not interested in young men? Why does she turn them all away? And what are you going to do about it?"

O-Toyo's father, who loved his daughter dearly, said only, "Well, well, she is still very young. There is time. There is no hurry. O-Toyo, my precious jewel, is still a child. See how she plays with her cat!"

"Ah, yes," replied the aunt. "Of course, Honorable Brother, you realize that the cat has bewitched your daughter and has cast a spell upon her, so that she will never love a young man. That is why he follows her so closely, day and night. And have you not heard of the Vampire Cat of Nabeshima, who bit a princess to death and then assumed her form? I say take this cat and kill it. Then O-Toyo will seek the companionship of her own kind."

"Aieeeeeee!" shrieked the father. "Can this

be? Certainly I have heard that tale, and others, but I assumed they were all nonsense!"

"One never knows," said his sister, cleverly.

After this, O-Toyo's father began to observe the two much more closely. The gentle, golden-eyed white cat, who had been brought up in the house since his kittenhood, had received nothing but love and kindness from O-Toyo. So he followed her, or sat in her lap, or sat quietly on a satin pillow in his corner, watching O-Toyo as she embroidered.

Nevertheless, the father was disturbed. He did not really believe the vampire cat story, "But still," he thought, "one never knows. If anything happened to O-Toyo . . ." He made up his mind to destroy the cat.

He went to O-Toyo and said, "My child, I am going to take the cat away and kill it. It follows you too closely. It has cast a spell upon you, which is why you have never loved any young man. And have you not heard of the Vampire Cat of Nabeshima?"

"Father, no!" cried O-Toyo. "Please do not be deluded by such nonsense! My dear Snowflake follows me only because he knows I love him! He is a gentle little cat! And surely you know that when I meet a young man I can be fond of, I will

marry. Why, you yourself have told me many, many times, that there is no hurry . . . Why are you blaming my little white cat? Father, I beg of you, do not believe the superstitions that people invent!"

Now her father, seeing the harmless little cat curled up asleep in his corner, suddenly felt very foolish. But to save his pride, he was determined to kill the pet, so he angrily drew out his sword.

O-Toyo screamed, quickly lifted the cat in her arms and ran out of the house. Wildly she ran on and on until she came to her father's granary. Panting, she hurried inside to hide and threw herself down on the floor behind some bags of grain.

A huge rat, twice the size of her cat, jumped out of a bag of grain, fell upon the girl and bit her. The brave and faithful Snowflake leaped at the monster with his claws and teeth and fought valiantly until he killed it. But the cat was seriously wounded. His soft white fur was covered with blood. O-Toyo crept over to her little pet and held him in her arms. He looked up at her, purred once, then closed his beautiful golden eyes forever.

O-Toyo wept bitterly.

When her father finally found her, she told him how her cat had fought and defended her.

"But now, father," she said, "I will never marry, and I will never live in your house again. I will spend my life atoning for your sin of stupidity."

O-Toyo retired to a convent. She never entered her father's house again, nor did she ever again look upon his face.

Her father banished his sister from his house. He wept constantly, for he missed the companionship of his lovely child. And he could never again look at any cat without feeling a pain in his heart. He grew old alone and never again did he blame an animal for superstitions invented by humans.

Folk Sayings from Around the World

Cats have never been ignored; people from all over the world have always had something to say about them.

Those who do not like cats
Will not get handsome mates.
                    —*Dutch Proverb*

He who owns a light-colored cat
        Will always have silver
He who owns a dark-colored cat
        Will always have gold.
                    —*Buddhist Saying*

Kiss the black cat
'Twill make ye fat
Kiss the white one
'Twill make ye lean.
            —*Old English Rhyme*

Cats of three colors
(black, brown and white)
bring good luck.
                        —*Japanese Sailors'*
                              Superstition

Four things are necessary for a home:
grain, a cock, a cat, and a wife.
                        —*Italian Saying*

Whenever the cat o' the house is black,
The lasses o' lovers will have no lack.
                        —*Scottish Rhyme*

If you carry a black cat to a place where five roads meet and then release him, the road he takes will lead you to buried treasure.

—French Superstition

Through the eyes of the cat you may see into another world.

—Irish Saying

If you want to be happy in a new home, a cat must move in with you.

—Russian Superstition

Notes on the Sources

Dividing the Cheese (Africa) was adapted from "Dividing the Cheese" in *Folk Tales of All Nations*, Lee, F. H., ed. New York: Tudor Publishing Company, 1946.

The Magic Ring (China and Korea) was adapted from two stories in *Nine Lives*, Briggs, Katharine M. New York: Pantheon, 1981.

Rhymes and Jingles (England) are in *Nursery Rhymes, Tales and Jingles*, Valentine, Mrs., ed. London: Frederick Warne and Company, c. 1886.

The Fox and the Cat (Russia) was adapted from "The Fox and the Cat" in *Folk Tales of All Nations*, Lee, F. H. (ed.) New York: Tudor Publishing Company, 1946.

The Pride of Schildburg (Germany) was adapted from "The Schildburgers" in *Folk Tales of All Nations*, Lee, F. H. (ed.) New York: Tudor Publishing Company, 1946, and from "The Lucky Cat" in *The Golden Bird: Folktales from Slovenia*, Kavcic, Vladimir. New York: World Publishing Company, 1969.

A LEGAL TAIL (Burma) was adapted from "The Tiger and the Cat" in *Burmese Law Tales: The Legal Element in Burmese Folklore*, Aung, Maung Htn. London: Oxford University Press, 1962. In Burmese society, a unique relationship existed between teacher and pupil, craftsman and apprentice. The pupil's service to the teacher could be revoked only under special circumstances. Folktales containing a riddle or problem were often used to illustrate a point of law.

A PLACE TO LIVE (Israel) was based on "The Cat's Allotment" in *Folktales of Israel*, Noy, Dov and Ben-Amos, Dan (eds.) Translated by Gene Baharav. Chicago: The University of Chicago Press. Toronto, Canada: The University of Toronto Press. London: Routledge and Kegan Paul, Ltd., 1963. Many different cultures meet in Israel and both the oldest and newest in folklore traditions can be found there. This tale was attributed to a Libyan source.

WHY THE CAT WASHES HIS PAWS AFTER EATING (Greece, after an Aesop fable.) in *All About Cats As Pets*, Zaum, Marjorie. New York: Julian Messner, 1981. Reprinted with permission of Simon and Schuster.

THE PRINCESS OF CATTENBORG (Sweden) was adapted from "Cattenborg" in *Swedish Fairy Tales*, Kaplan, Irma. Chicago: New York: Follett Publishing Company, 1967 and from "The Earl of Cattenborough" in *European Folk and Fairy Tales*, Jacobs, Joseph. New York: G. P. Putnam's Sons, 1916. "Puss in Boots" is probably the best known of this type of story.

FOLK SAYINGS (United States-Midwest) in *Folklore from Adams County, Illinois*, Hyatt, Harry M. New York: Memoirs of the Alma Egan Hyatt Foundation, 1935.

COUNT GATTO (Italy) was adapted from "The House of Cats" in *The House of Cats and Other Stories*, Hampden, John. New York: Farrar, Straus & Giroux, 1967 and from "The Fable of the Cats" in *Italian Fables*, Calvino, Italo. New York: Orion Press, 1959.

THE FAITHFUL CAT (Japan) was adapted from "The Story of the Faithful Cat" in *Tales of Old Japan*, Redesdale, Lord. G.C.V.D., K.C.B. London: Macmillan and Company, Ltd., The Caravan Library, 1928. First published 1871.

FOLK SAYINGS FROM AROUND THE WORLD (Old English rhyme, Scottish rhyme, Dutch proverb) in *The Velvet Paw*, Conger, Jean. New York: Ivan Obolensky, Inc., 1963. (Buddhist saying, French superstition) in *Cult of the Cat*, Dale-Green, Patricia. New York: Tower Publications, Inc., 1963. Originally published by Houghton Mifflin Company. (Japanese sailor's superstition, Italian saying) in *The Tiger in the House*, Van Vechten, Carl. New York: Alfred A. Knopf, 1936.

Bibliography

Aung, Maung Htn. *Burmese Law Tales: The Legal Element in Burmese Folklore.* London: Oxford University Press, 1962.

Briggs, Katharine M. *Nine Lives.* New York: Pantheon Books, 1980.

Calvino, Italo. *Italian Fables.* New York: Orion Press, 1959.

Conger, Jean. *The Velvet Paw.* New York: Ivan Obolensky, 1963.

Dale-Green, Patricia. *Cult of the Cat.* New York: Tower Publications, Inc., 1963. Originally published by Houghton Mifflin Company.

Hampden, John. *The House of Cats and Other Stories.* New York: Farrar, Straus & Giroux, 1967.

Hyatt, Harry M. *Folklore from Adams County, Illinois.* New York: Memoirs of the Alma Egan Hyatt Foundation, 1935.

Jacobs, Joseph. *European Folk and Fairy Tales*. New York: G. P. Putnam's Sons, 1916.

Kaplan, Irma. *Swedish Fairy Tales*. Chicago, New York: Follett Publishing Company, 1967.

Kavcic, Vladimir. *The Golden Bird: Folktales from Slovenia*. New York: World Publishing Company, 1969.

Lee, F. H., ed. *Folktales of All Nations*. New York: Tudor Publishing Company, 1946.

Lowry, Shirley Park. *Familiar Mysteries: The Truth in Myth*. New York, Oxford: Oxford University Press, 1982.

Mooney, Samantha. *A Snowflake in My Hand*. New York: Delacorte Press/Eleanor Friede, 1983.

Noy, Dov, and Ben-Amos, Dan, eds. *Folktales of Israel*. Translated by Gene Baharav. Chicago: The University of Chicago Press. Toronto, Canada: The University of Toronto Press. London: Routledge and Kegan Paul, Ltd., 1963.

Redesdale, Lord, G.C.V.D., K.C.B. *Tales of Old Japan*. London: Macmillan and Company, Ltd., The Caravan Library, 1928. First published 1871.

Valentine, Mrs., ed. *Nursery Rhymes, Tales and Jingles*. London: Frederick Warne and Company, c. 1886.

Van Vechten, Carl. *The Tiger in the House*. New York: Alfred A. Knopf, 1936.

Zaum, Marjorie. *All About Cats As Pets*. New York: Julian Messner, 1981.